The Life of a Child
That Should Have Been
a **Boy** or a Girl

The Life of a Child That Should Have Been a **Boy** or a Girl

Verrilien Clerve MSN

iUniverse, Inc.
New York   Bloomington

iUniverse books may be ordered through booksellers or by contacting:

iUniverse
1663 Liberty Drive
Bloomington, IN 47403
www.iuniverse.com
1-800-Authors (1-800-288-4677)

ISBN: 978-1-4401-2087-9 (pbk)
ISBN: 978-1-4401-2088-6 (ebk)

Printed in the United States of America

iUniverse rev. date: 1/19/2009

To Manouska and family; all hermaphrodites; all transgender individuals; and all other sexes who struggle daily to live a normal life in our society.

I acknowledge Widwant Kaur for her support.

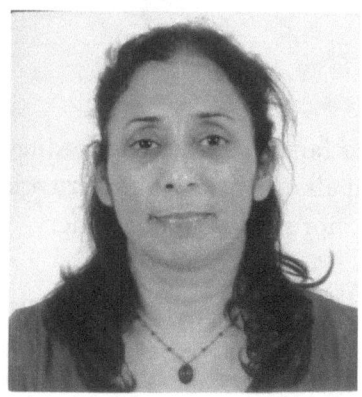

Preface

Life defines itself in many ways. No one knows how one's life will turn out. Everyone has to face the journey of life, but there is a price before reaching that journey. For some, the journey of life holds many meanings, and for others, it holds none. No matter the circumstances, no one can know one's destiny from the day one is born. This book is about a hermaphroditic child who should have been a boy or a girl. One can learn many lessons from this true story.

Chapter One

Sexual identity is very important for many. This is the way most of us classify males and females. However, the magnitude of gender is not essential among infants, but the behavior people expect of boys and girls is set in action patterns that will prolong for an era. As the child grows up, he or she will discover his or her sexual identity by interacting with peers and experimenting with the opposite sex.

As a way of life, we obey the rules of our parents and authorities. Many times, children seem to be forced to measure up to adult expectations in all areas of life. Some parents even try to tell them how to act and how not to act. Some ways of life are acceptable for some. Many people view hermaphrodites as a threat to society.

Let me elaborate on the issues of family. What is a family? A typical family is a group that shares the same norm and culture. Many of the tribulations folks face begin with unwholesome family life.

Chapter Two

The city of San Marco is known for its beaches, exotic birds, and craggy mountains. The people in the city are very happy. Every day, tourists visit the city in great numbers to see the beaches and the exotic birds that make the city well known. However, a few miles down the beach, a family had to deal with a big secret. What is the secret?

In the city, most pregnant women do not go to the hospital when they go into labor. Instead, midwives deliver most babies. Among all the babies that were delivered, one was a hermaphrodite.

The Peacocks were a typical family but their lives changed with the birth of their first child. The Peacock family had no idea what it meant to be hermaphrodite. They accepted the newborn as it was. Neighbors and friends came to see the family and asked the question many of us ask a family with a newborn. Is it a girl or a boy? The mother said it was a girl. The father did not say anything, but something was not right.

The family named the baby Manouska, which is a girl's name. Nobody in the neighborhood knew that the baby was part girl and part boy. The Peacocks had a hard time dressing the baby—one day the baby's mother would dress him or her as a boy, and the next day, she would dress him or her as a girl.

Some people posed questions to which they could not find any answers. Some asked if there was something wrong with the family. Neighbors, friends, and families were curious because of the clothes that the baby wore. Some were amazed by the reaction of the family, and some waited to see what the child would become in the years to come.

As the child grew up, things changed for the family.

Chapter Three

Manouska could act like a boy one day, and like a little princess the next day. The child's parents bought two different kinds of toys: boys' and girls' toys. In our society, when baby boys are born, they are bought trucks and dinosaurs and everything is blue. When baby girls are born, it is the exact opposite; everything is pink, and the toys consist of dolls and ballerinas.

When a girl walks through a toy store, that girl is drawn to toys that are wrapped in pinks and purples and have frills and daisies. On the other hand, a boy is drawn to toys that are blue and green. Typically, the toys that a girl plays with encourage caring for babies and cooking and cleaning. The toys that a boy plays with are trucks and construction vehicles and tools, which encourage very masculine behaviors.

Toys that are geared towards both boys and girls are typically only toys that encourage learning or that motivate one to better oneself. However, Manouska's parents bought two different types of toys with blue colors and pink colors. The child continued to grow.

Manouska's parents started blaming each other for the child's gender. They consulted health care professionals and others in order to find ways to cope with their tragedy. At six years old, Manouska began to play with others boys but not girls.

Manouska's mother was unhappy about Manouska playing with other boys, but his or her father was very happy about it. Manouska's preference for friends who were boys caused confusion in the family. Manouska did not wear girls' clothes when going to school, and his or her father was happy because his wish was to have a boy.

The child began to play with children whose families were very suspicious of the child's gender. Some said, "This child played like a boy, and we thought she was a girl." Despite the tension, Manouska's parents devoted themselves to teach the child good manners like how to say "thank you."

At age six, Manouska began to display certain behaviors like biting or kicking other children. Many parents in the neighborhood were worried about Manouska's behavior, and they expressed their concerns to Manouska's parents.

One day, Manouska resembled a boy and the next day a girl. Many in the neighborhood suspected that the child had gender problems and that the child's parents kept it secret. It was a life like no other.

Chapter Four

The child's parent wanted to move to a different city, because they did not want the child to experience hardship due to his or her gender. However, they joined a therapy session with the child in order to avoid gender confusion as the child grew up. In the last therapy session, the sex therapist advised them to tell neighbors and family about the child's gender, which would help the child accept one gender or another. The family was in turmoil.

One day at a neighborhood meeting, Manouska's parents wanted to tell the neighbors about the child's gender. But they wondered how the neighbors receive the news? Before the meeting, the hosts called Manouska's parents to invite them to talk about the child's gender. Manouska's mother began to cry as she and her husband approached the podium to speak to all of their neighbors.

Manouska's father refused to speak, but the mother began by saying, "First, my husband and I would like to apologize for the secret that we kept from you for six years." She continued, "I know that all of you are my friends, my families, and my neighbors. I know you have supported my husband and me. Now I want to tell you about our child. When our child was born, we were confused because the child was born a hermaphrodite. We want to tell you about that to stop gossip and suspicion."

After she finished speaking, many of their neighbors stood up and expressed their feelings. Some apologized for their behavior, and some were frustrated because of the secret the family had kept from them for six years. Many felt betrayed by the family. However, close family remained supportive of Manouska's parents.

The news spread all over the neighborhood. Everywhere the Peacocks went, people were discussing the child's sexual gender. How did some people see the child and his/her parents? What was the problem with the child sexual orientation?

Many people worried because the child could like boys or girls. The sex of the child concerned some people, and many gossiped about that situation day and night.

Chapter Five

What is hermaphrodite? The term hermaphrodite refers to a human being with a combination of female and male internal and external genitalia. It is the union of the two sexes in the same individual or the combination of some of their characteristics or organs in one individual.

A hermaphrodite is sexually unfinished or partly male and partly female. Due to the similarities between male and female sex organs, it may be difficult to tell whether a human hermaphrodite is a female with an overdeveloped clitoris or a male with an underdeveloped penis, cleft scrotum, and undescended testes.

Manouska's parents wanted to move to a different city because of the reactions of their neighbors, but others advised them to stay. The child continued to attend school despite the way other kids treated him/her. The child liked to play with colors, ride his or her bicycle, and play sports—things other kids like to do. Manouska would go home after school, pick up a piece of white legal paper and some colored pencils, and start drawing pictures of anything that came to his/her mind. His/her mother liked to congratulate him/her on his/her drawing. The father would pick up a ball and call for Manouska to play with him.

Chapter Six

Every Wednesday, the family took the child to see the family psychiatrist. One day the psychiatrist advised the family to let the child be himself/herself. The psychiatrist counseled the family not to confuse the child. Doing so would cause identity problems as the child grew up.

On the way back home from the appointment, Manouska's parents started arguing about the child's gender. Understand that Manouska parents were very superstitious. Manouska's mother told her husband that the reason that Manouska's gender was confused was because he used to wear her clothes and she used to say that that their boy might be like him one day.

"Now our child is half boy and half girl."

"You are too superstitious," her husband said, "and perhaps Manouska got it from one of your family's genes or heredity."

This day was like no other, and Manouska cried to see his/her parents arguing. Both parents stopped arguing, and Manouska's mother also began to cry.

Hermaphroditic life is hard for society to accept. Some see it as abnormal, and others see it as a natural part of humanity. After all this, the family began to reflect on the child's sexual identity.

"We cannot raise this child alone," the father told the mother. "We need outside help, like church-based community, family, and friends."

Chapter Seven

At age seven, the child began to experience certain changes, like developing muscle. Some of parents in the neighborhood watch Manouska playing with their kids and they were not happy. Sometimes Manouska had to play alone after school because other children's parents refused to let their kids play with him/her.

At that age, Manouska started playing more with boy's toys, which was what his/her father wanted and expected.

However, his/her mother wanted him/her to play with girls' toys. Despite these preferences, the family stopped living in denial. They finally accepted the fact that their child was different from other children.

In school, Manouska experienced intense loneliness and self-hatred because of his/her sexual gender. Some kids taunted Manouska by saying things like "Are you a girl or a boy? You need to find your own kind to play with." Manouska tried to fit in and be accepted by others, but the lack of support and role models in school left him/her feeling alone and ashamed. Manouska sometimes skipped classes because of verbal aggravation from other kids and from some of the teachers who sometimes joked about his/her sexual gender. Manouska was trying to find his/her place in the neighborhood and at school by playing with other kids.

Growing up as a hermaphrodite was very difficult. He/she continuously had to find a way to try to be a normal kid who played with other kids in school. Sometimes, Manouska feared that no other kids would like to play with him/her and that he/she would not be accepted. One day, Manouska asked his/her mother, "Why do other kids refuse to play with me?"

Manouska's mother said, "Some of the kids have been told by their parents that you are not the same as they are. And you were born differently. For some in the neighborhood, being a hermaphrodite is a disease or a plague that could affect other kids."

Manouska's parents felt the attitudes of families and friends would affect their child's well being. They felt the type of prejudices toward them because some friends and neighbors felt that the child should stay out of their neighborhoods. Others felt that a hermaphrodite child should not be allowed to go to the same school as other children.

The child's parents lacked support from their own families. The associations within their family were completely changed. For instance, Manouska's grandparents stopped visiting his/her house for fear that others might treat them like outcasts.

The saga continued, and Manouska turned eight.

Chapter Eight

When the family went camping during the summer, a few kids at the summer camp started calling out to Manouska, "Hey, boy, or hey, girl." Manouska cried and his/her parents had to leave the camp early to go home. The camping had been a way to celebrate Manouska's birthday, but that day was a sad one for the whole family.

During that summer, the family visited another city to find out whether they could relocate or not. They spent half of the summer in a city where they were barely known. A few days before school opened, the family took the child shopping. While they were all at the department store, they saw other kids with their parents.   After they finished shopping, they went home, and the family discussed their plan and the future of their child.

Manouska's father expressed his ideas: "When Manouska turns ten years old, we should move to a different city."

Although Manouska's parents accepted him/her as a hermaphrodite, other families made the family feel unwanted in the neighborhood. Manouska's parents never stopped taking him/her to a psychiatrist for counseling. Manouska sometimes discussed his/her feelings with the psychiatrist, expressing his/her anger at the way others treated him/her.

After seeing the psychiatrist, Manouska transferred to a different school located in the same city. During the first week of school, Manouska sat closed to another student who introduced himself to Manouska. They played together, and Manouska was finally happy to find someone who could play with him/her without any prejudiced remarks.

As the child was attending a different school, the school offered therapy two days a week. One day while in therapy session, Manouska's mother began to cry.

"Manouska is my child, and I will do whatever it takes to help her," she said. "The only fear I have," said the mother "is that my own family won't accept the child. It is very hard for me and my husband."

The new school also provided after-school activities where Manouska could play with other kids. All of these activities helped the child psychologically and emotionally, boosting the child's self-esteemwww.sirius.com, according to the school psychologist. In the neighborhood, people wondered about the future of the child. Some continued to ask, "Would he/she grow up to be a man or a woman?"

From age six to eight, Manouska's life, and those of his/her parents, was a nightmare. Neighbors, friends, and families still rejected the child's gender, and many were afraid of the child's activities with other kids. A few months before Manouska turned nine, families, friends, and neighbors had a meeting about what had happened in the neighborhood during the previous two years. Many decided to accept the child's sexual gender, but some were still not convinced that Manouska could be a normal child.

Chapter Nine

One night, when Manouska was nine, he/she woke up crying. His/her parents rushed into the child's room to find out what had happened. When they got into the room, they saw Manouska sitting at the edge of the bed crying.

"Manouska, what's wrong?" his/her mother asked.

"Nothing, Mummy," Manouska said. "You are crying," said his/her mother.

Finally, Manouska told his/ her parents that he/ she was scared and he/she would like to sleep in the same room with his/ her parents.

At that age, Manouska began to play with both boys and girls, and he/she displayed certain talents. One of them was running. Manouska loved to run, and he/she won the school racing competition. She also played clarinet for the school band. Many teachers and other students developed close relationships with Manouska.

The same year, Manouska grandparents came to see him/her. At that time, his/her grandparents asked for forgiveness and told the family how the people who lived in their neighborhood had influenced their decision not to come to see Manouska. However, others in the neighborhood let their kids play with Manouska.

Through church outreach, the family learned that Manouska was not the only transgender child in the community—there were five more hermaphrodites. Some people in the church formed a committee to help Manouska and his/her parents cope with the situation, connecting them with other parents of hermaphrodite children.

Despite of all of the progress in the neighborhood and at school, Manouska's parents intended to move from their original city when Manouska turned ten, because the family still lived in fear of hatred from others. One day in a church meeting, the family expressed their concerns and asked church members to help them with Manouska because no one understood his/her pain or what he/she was going through. Manouska's mother said that people needed to stop calling Manouska "homo" or "abnormal." For a nine year old who has no life experience and doesn't know how to deal with issues, name calling can crush his/her spirit.

The school's headmaster decided to meet with all students, teachers, and others in order to discuss hermaphrodites.

"Hermaphrodite children not only face unhindered prejudice and aggravation at school," he began by saying, "they also sometimes face similar treatment from others in their neighborhoods. Many times these children are abhorred instead of approved of. Such treatment sometimes leaves them with nowhere to turn.

"I believe it is time to stop these behaviors and begin a healing process in the neighborhood where these children reside." The head master went on to say, "All teachers need to support all children despite their sexual gender. All teachers need to be role models to those children. Teachers should not joke about these children, and all teachers are expected to make positive remarks about them. A teacher who takes a stand against those who harass and discriminate against a student due to his or her gender can make a difference. All teachers need to give positive information in the classrooms and outside the classrooms." The headmaster closed by saying, "Let's build a future for all children."

Manouska no longer faced harassment and threats at his/her school. Everybody learned to accept her gender. Manouska and other hermaphrodite children received fair treatment from everybody at school. The year was almost over, and Manouska was about to turn ten.

Chapter Ten

When Manouska turned ten, the family took him/her camping because he/she loved to camp. While camping, Manouska went fishing, went horseback riding, learned how to make certain toys like motorcycles, mailboxes, and more. Then one month before the beginning of the school year, the family went to visit the city that they planned to move to. While en route to the city, Manouska asked his/her parents if he/she could stay in the city of San Marco where he/she was born. His/her father told him/her that some people who lived in San Marco were not too friendly and that they had to move to a different city.

"However," said the father, "you can go back after you finish school."

While they were in the city, Manouska had the chance to go to the city fair for kids. It was a happy day for the family, and they stayed in the city for the entire month until they went back to San Marco to pack their belongings for the move.

Before leaving San Marco, Manouska and his/her parents visited old friends and families to let them know that they were moving to a different city. Many in the neighborhood were astounded to see them leaving. Some were cheerless and some were blissful. Most wondered what Manouska's life would be like in a different city.

When the family arrived at their destination, new neighbors welcomed them to the neighborhood. A few days after they moved, Manouska started going to his/her new school. Manouska spent at least a few months adjusting to the new school. Within six months after the move, Manouska met new friends at his/her school, and many others appreciated his/her talent. He/she signed up to play clarinet for the school band and became part of the track team. There were also after school activities like biking, cookery, and more. Manouska was interested in cooking. After school, she stayed in order to learn how to make pastry and more.

The school also provided therapy sessions for hermaphrodite students and others, but the family did not share the secret about their child with the neighbors. As Manouska grew up, he/she interacted with other boys. The family did not pay any attention to that behavior because they thought that Manouska simply liked to play with boys rather than with girls.

Years passed, and Manouska continued to play with boys. It wasn't until age fifteen that Manouska's family began paying more attention to his/her behavior.

Chapter Eleven

At fifteen, Manouska started wearing his/her mother's clothes. His/her parents didn't know that he/she was wearing female clothes until one day when Manouska went out with friends and he/she wore female clothes and makeup. His /her father was devastated after seeing that behavior. He told Manouska not to dress like a woman. However, his/her mother supported Manouska's behavior. The next day, the family decided to go back to the family psychiatrist, who started interviewing Manouska.

"When did you start wearing a woman's dress?" the psychiatrist asked.

"When I was fifteen," Manouska said.

"What made you want to wear women's clothes?"

"I have never felt like a boy, and I do not know why I am like this. I think it is because of my sexual gender."

"Manouska, sometimes people with your sexual gender can be called maggots, but you do not have to feel that way. You have a great future in front of you. Do things that make you happy, not things that make others happy."

After the interview, the psychiatrist told the family to accept his/her behavior and not to pressure him/her to act differently. Every day, Manouska went to school dressed in a different way. One day, he/she dressed as a man, and the next day, he/she dressed as a woman.

Many people accepted his/her behavior. But some at his/her school laughed and were astonished by his/her behavior.

Chapter Twelve

By seventeen, Manouska was almost finished with high school. All the years Manouska had spent in San Marco overflowed with extreme seclusion, trepidation, and self-hatred despite many who had close relationships with him/her. As he/she came close to finishing high school, he/she experienced a different lifestyle. In San Marco, Manouska had tried to fit in, but in the city of San Juan many accepted his/her sexual gender with no discrimination.

One day, some students held a meeting to discuss the lives of transgender students in the community and school. The guest speaker spoke about the lives of hermaphrodites in the area. The guest speaker explained that others should not be afraid of a person's sexual gender. Being different did not mean that one should be discriminated against. The community should support hermaphrodite students, and everyone had a role to play.

After the meeting, Manouska went home and described to his/her parents what he/she had heard in the school meeting. His/her father was very pleased with the meeting.

Throughout the year, Manouska wanted to gain autonomy from his/her family, even though he/she still needed their support and leadership. He/she attended many hermaphrodite student meetings alone. These meetings provided resources that Manouska needed in order to live a normal life. The high school also provided after-school activities for many transgender students. For instance, there were social clubs where transgender students could discuss their social issues, and the school provided counseling sessions for the students. All of these helped Manouska's sexual development.

At that age, Manouska preferred to be with his/her peers rather than his/her parents. He/she sought advice from others rather than his/her parents. As a seventeen-year-old, Manouska explored his/her sexual identity and started dating boys and sometimes girls.

Manouska sexual orientation aggravated some people in the community. Some wondered if he/she would be normal or if he/she would survive his/her lifestyle. Others gossiped among themselves. Despite all of the programs offered by the school, many were skeptical about his/her lifestyle. Some argued that his/her lifestyle could influence others to become like him/her.

Manouska's father was happy when he/she dated girls, and his/her mother was the opposite.

Chapter Thirteen

At eighteen, Manouska entered his/her senior year of high school. That year wasn't like any other. Manouska got involved in many programs, such as a program counseling other students about their sexual orientation as transgender individuals and the school election of a prom king and queen. Many high school seniors and lower classmen were happy with Manouska's professionalism and the way he/she handled many situations that involved other students. For instance, one hermaphrodite student feared that he/she would not be able to have a normal life after school. Manouska invited the student to the transgender counseling session in order to find ways to cope with his/her sexual gender. Teachers, the schoolmaster, students, and many parents were also very pleased with Manouska's ability to help others.

Three months before graduation, Manouska had a big party. The purpose of the party was to invite high school students to come together to support hermaphrodite students. Many students passed around flyers for the party that read: All transgender, homosexual, and heterosexuals are invited for a soirée de gala to support each other. a lot of people showed up to support hermaphrodite students and others. During the party, Manouska gave a speech to a crowd of 150 students.

"Friends, teachers, and families: in three months, we graduate. Some of us will go to different paths. Some will get married. Some will go to college. And some will not marry. Let me tell you—when I was little, my parents fought over my gender. One wanted a boy and the other a girl. Even though my dad still wants me to be a boy, he has accepted me the way I am," said Manouska. He/she continued to say, "You all know that I am a hermaphrodite, and I am happy to be. I accept the fact that there are others like me who support me. Let us not be discouraged. The school has provided support for all of us. If some of you need help, do not hesitate to go to the counseling center." He/she closed by saying, "Have fun everybody."

At the end of the party, thy held a candlelight vigil in order to remember many hermaphrodite students who lived in fear and many who were deceased.

Chapter Fourteen

Manouska was one of several students involved in the prom. He/she helped to decorate the high school ballroom, and helped with the selection of the prom king and queen. After doing all this, he/she went home to get ready for the prom event.

Around seven o'clock, Manouska went to the prom, accompanied by many other hermaphrodite students as well as his/her parents. It was a prom night to remember. That night the prom band played a song entitled "Can we ever say good-bye." After the song, Manouska was chosen to crown the prom king and queen. He/she was also chosen to give the prom speech, and it sounded like this:

"Fellow students, this is our last night to be together. We have come a long way, and the time has come to say goodbye to some. The future is in our hands. Whatever we set our minds to, I believe we can do it. You are the future of our society. Many parents are proud of you tonight. My parents are here with me, and I am very proud and fortunate to have them by my side. Most of you know my sexual gender, and I am proud as a hermaphrodite. Most of us stand here tonight because of good support from friends, teachers, classmates, parents, and the community. In short, I want to thank you for all your support and wish you all Godspeed."

Many were in tears after Manouska's speech, and they wished each other good luck.

Chapter Fifteen

On the day of his/her high school graduation Manouska woke up early to prepare for the graduation ceremony at four o'clock. That day many friends, families, and neighbors from San Marco came to celebrate. Some brought gifts, and others just came to support Manouska.

During that day, there was a problem because Manouska didn't know what to wear. He/she finally called his/her mother for advice. Manouska's mother told him/her to "wear whatever you would like to wear." That day Manouska wore a black suit.

At the graduation, the schoolmaster and other teachers were there to congratulate students. There were also many guest speakers at the graduation, and Manouska was one of them. Manouska gave a speech entitled "The Future Is in Your Hands," and the speech sounded like this:

"Today my friends we close one chapter and open another. We hold the future in our hands. Most of us will experience key transitions in our lives. Some will go to college; some will get married; and some will go to work after high school. Regardless of where each of us goes after high school, we are connected as friends and families. High school was the beginning of our future. Each of us will deal with constructive and destructive events in our life, but we can come out of those events as winners not losers. Many people in the community count on us to carry on the torch. Let us fulfill our dreams for those who will come after us. Thank you."

After the ceremony, Manouska's parents and friends took pictures together. On the way home, Manouska's father asked him/her what was next.

"I am going to college to be a teacher," he/she answered.

The same year, Manouska received a letter of acceptance from one of the universities in the city. The letter stated:

We have established your submission for undergraduate study at the University. Because of large quantity of applicants this year, rivalry is sturdy, but providentially, we have recommended you for acceptance. To uphold our students blissful, the college offers many activities that will accommodate your needs. It seems that you probably may not have adequate information to make a jingle choice. The enclosed handout will provide a meticulous depiction of our Educational Program. Since other eligible students are on a waiting roll for entrance, please inform me in writing of your choice as soon as possible.

Chapter Sixteen

College life can be difficult because of transitions that many have to make. It presents many challenges for many. Manouska was apprehensive about not only his/her achievement at college but also his/her communal and emotional adjustment as well. He/she felt anxious, wondering if he/she would fit in or not.

However, Manouska adapted to the changes very quickly. During his/her first year, Manouska had to face many obstacles. As a hermaphrodite, Manouska faced prejudice and discrimination from other students. He/ she felt degraded as a person. Some students called him/her names, such as "hey, sissy" or "hey, abnormal." The feelings of rejection were real, and Manouska refuse to go to some classes.

For the first semester, Manouska felt isolated at the college. One day, Manouska went to the counseling center to talk to someone at the college about his/her fear. To help Manouska conquer his/her fear, the university counselor suggested that Manouska join a hermaphrodite support group at the college. The support group met three days a week.

On the college campus, there were many with brochures to promote social interactions among the students regardless of gender. These brochures were distributed to students inviting them to come out and speak up about their sexual gender. After speaking to the counselor, one day Manouska went to one of the meetings and found many support groups. The university provided special student organizations for hermaphrodites, transgender, homosexual, and heterosexual students to help them understand their sexuality in a more specific way. At the college, many students were ready to help other students who were attending the college for the first time and who had hard time coping with their genders.

At the university, Manouska developed adult relationships with others, and assimilated his/her approach and attitudes in his/her typical days. Manouska overcame his/her fear by being more open about his/her gender. Manouska began to accept his/her sexual gender more openly than he/she had in high school. He/she changed his/her attitudes toward other students who treated him/her unfairly and began to interact with others at the university.

Talking about sexual gender was difficult for Manouska as a freshman in college. In order to overcome his/her fear, he/she sought out positive resources like group support.

Chapter Seventeen

During his/her second year in college, Manouska met a girl whom he/she was interested in. It was difficult for Manouska to let himself/herself like a girl because of his/her sexual identity, but Manouska liked to make Joanna happy.

Many of his/her college friends kept his/her sexuality secret. Despite the way that he/she treated the girl, his/her feminine side prevented him/her from going further. One day, Joanna asked Manouska to take her home from something. When they arrived home, Manouska told Joanna that he/she was a hermaphrodite and that he/she could not have a normal relationship with her.

Joanna replied by saying, "Manouska, I know you are a hermaphrodite." She went on to say, "We might not have a normal relationship, but we could be friends." They never had an intimate relationship, but they remained friends for life.

The second year of college was not as difficult as the first year, as Manouska adjusted to college life and his/her sexual gender. During that year, he/she continued to attend support group meeting. One day, the host of the meeting asked if anyone had a question or would like to comment on anything before the meeting adjourned. Manouska stood up and said, "My name is Manouska, and I've been attending this group for over six months." He/she further said that she was grateful for all the support she had received from many of them. After saying all this, he/she offered to help at the next meeting.

One day there was a student rally where Manouska was the primary speaker. He/she began by saying, "People with different genders come here to get educated not to be scrutinized. Students like us (hermaphrodites, transgender, homosexuals, and other sexual genders) should not live in fear. We need to respect each other's autonomy." He/ she continued to say that the college provided a lot of support for hermaphrodites and other genders. "All of us need to be active and help pave the way for people who may be having a harder time than us. Being a hermaphrodite is not rewarding in many societies. To carry on in society, hermaphrodites need strong support from other groups."

Students came in large numbers to support the hermaphrodites, transgender students, and homosexuals. After the meeting, some vowed not to discriminate against other sexes. Manouska was very active during his/her second year of college in making other college students aware of the situation. The most important capacity Manouska possessed was to influence others. He/she helped other students not to fear their own sexual identities.

Chapter Eighteen

During Manouska's third year of college, he/she devoted most of his/her time to studying and counseling other students about their own sexual genders. Manouska founded a support group entitled the "Sexual Identity Support Group."

The first time the group met, Manouska explained to the group that sexual orientation used to be a big concern for many at the college. However, now the college had assorted resources for people who are hermaphrodites, homosexuals, and transgender individuals. Many heterosexual students provided support to Manouska's group. Manouska went on to say that college is a refuge for everyone.

"Some of us do not have any support at home. I am fortunate enough to have my parents with me," said Manouska. "All of you know that education is one of the ways to overcome trepidation, so please do not hesitate to talk to people about their sexual orientations."

After the meeting, Manouska distributed brochures to all students who attended the support group meeting.

During the same year, Manouska's father died suddenly after having a heart attack. When Manouska got the news, he/she was devastated. Many students and friends came to support him/her. Manouska left school and returned home for his/her father's funeral. When he/she arrived at home, his/her mother and families were inconsolable.

Manouska helped his/her mother arrange the funeral. On the day of the funeral, current and former classmates accompanied him/her to the funeral. After the funeral, Manouska stayed with his/her mother for over a month. However, his/her mother advised her to go back to school and finish his/her program.

When he/she returned to the college, a large amount of students—hermaphrodites, heterosexuals, and homosexuals—came to support him/her and turned to him/her for help and assistance. Some were dealing with anxiety, depression, thoughts of suicide, and relationships issues. Most of the students attended the sexual identity support group Manouska had started for counseling. Manouska mentored some students on how to help others with sexual gender issues.

During Manouska's fourth year in college, there was a rally on campus about violence against gay students. Manouska decided to give a speech to the crowd about gay violence on campus. The speech went like this:

"My friends, in few months, I will graduate from college, and I will be integrated in the workforce. Even though education may change my life, I will still be a hermaphrodite. The community will judge others and me as being different. Hermaphrodite, gay, transgender—none of these are diseases or epidemics; they are sexual identities. I don't think we should be judged because of sexual difference."

After the speech, many gave testimonies of prejudice and discrimination that they had experienced on campus.

The first testimony was given by a gay student: "I was beaten by some students after they discovered that I am gay. Some of the college police were on the scene when two students beat me up and cut the tires of my car."

The second testimony also came from a gay student: "Some students called me all types of names on campus. Others harassed me until I dropped one of my classes."

The third testimony was from a hermaphroditic student: "I lived in fear for over one year. Many forced me to leave my dormitory after I told my roommate that I was a hermaphrodite."

The fourth testimony came from a hermaphroditic student: "I was stabbed after I told some students about my sexual orientation."

The fifth testimony also came from a hermaphroditic student: "I received threatening phone calls from unknown students, and I had to move out of my apartment."

The sixth testimony was also from a hermaphroditic student: "I was sodomized by some students one night because of my gender."

The seventh testimony was given by a gay student: "One student harassed me in the school cafeteria and spat in my food because of my sexual preference."

The eighth testimony was from transgender student: "Some students tore my books because of my sexual identity."

In the rally, a transgender student said that he was currently undergoing hormone treatments and receiving silicone injections to help him develop breasts and a more feminine shape. He had gotten a name change and no longer went by a "boy name" at all. No one even knew what it was. He lived as a male at the college, but outside of school, he lived as a female.

After all testimonies, Manouska explained to the group that there were support groups available to help students come to term with their genders. As a hermaphrodite, Manouska could act one day as male and the next day as a female. Friends and families supported him/her because they knew that he/she was a hermaphrodite.

Chapter Nineteen

Two months before his/her college graduation, Manouska found a teaching job with the high school he/she had attended.

Manouska received a letter from the high school's administrative office stating: "Dear Manouska Peacock, this letter is to inform you that we gladly accept you as one of our teachers, and we are looking forward to working with you."

On the day of graduation Manouska's family, friends, and neighbors went to support and congratulate him/her on his/her achievement. Manouska was the first to graduate from college in his/her family. After the ceremony, Manouska and his/her family took graduation pictures.

Later that same day, there was a big party at Manouska's parent house where everyone celebrated his/her college achievement. Manouska's mother reminder him/her that his/her dad would be proud if he were alive.

Manouska went back to live with his/her mother since the high school where he/she had gotten a teaching job was closed to the house. Before starting his/her new job, Manouska went to visit some friends and families in San Marco. He/she spent two weeks there. While being there, Manouska became friends with some who had despised him/her because of his/her hermaphroditic gender.

Chapter Twenty

Manouska started his/her teaching career at age twenty-two. He/she decided to teach a sexuality class. This class curriculum explained, in detail, why the students needed the sexuality class. Such details included: "Sexuality is a huge element of our lives, but it is not discussed openly in our school and community. Students need to explore their sexualities by asking questions." The majority of the contents covered the definition of sexuality.

According to Manouska, one objective of the class was to enhance each student's ability to think and make good decisions about what to do or what to believe about sexual identity.

On the first day of class, many high school students, including seniors, registered to take the class. That day many parents came to listen to what Manouska was teaching their children.

Manouska began by saying that "parents play a big role in the lives of their children, and sex education should not be hidden from the kids." He/she went on to say, "Many parents might not agree with many of us about sexual education, but it will help many students to explore their sexual identity in a positive way." Because of Manouska's sexual orientation, many parents were afraid that Manouska would give their kids wrong information about sex.

"Sexual education encourages the spiritual, moral, cultural, mental, and physical development of many of us. Teaching children to learn and understand human sexuality is a mechanism to a healthy sexual relationship. The responsibility of teachers and parents is to work together to teach children."

Chapter Twenty-One

At age twenty-three, Manouska offered after-school help to other hermaphrodite, homosexual, and transgender students. One day, a gay student approached Manouska after class and explained to him/her that he wanted to commit suicide because his parents had disowned him after he had declared that he was gay. After receiving the news, Manouska began to cry and invited the gay student to stay at his/her house. The next day, Manouska started passing fliers around for a big high school gathering for hermaphrodites, transgender, and gay students. The gathering started with a big speech that went like this:

"Whether we like it or not, sexual characteristics are unavoidable. Some of us are born with our sexual identity; some have changed their gender; and some have adopted a different lifestyle. Despite sexual identity, we need to respect and accept others. Many gay youths have thoughts of suicide or commit suicide because of lack of support from their loved ones. Gay students deal with turmoil and instability of emotions because of peer pressure and more. Gay people are the most discriminated against and the most suicidal people in school. Suicidal belief and attempts are common among gay students, due to high levels of tension caused by many parents' narrow-minded view of homosexuality.

"This pressure is more compounded by the verity that gay youth often feel powerless to talk about their tribulations with associates and relatives. Much of the ache, unfriendliness, and desperate feelings experienced by gay youth could be stopped if parents accepted their kids as they are."

After the speech by Manouska, a gay student presented a speech, and he started by saying, "It is not everyday that I stand up in front of group like this. Now I must tell you, my friends, that I have suffered a lot. Being gay when living under your family's roof is difficult for many of us. In order to overcome their initial destructive reaction, I had to seek help from other friends and family members.

"Many parents do not know how to react to a gay child's behavior. First my parents disowned me. Because of my parents' reactions, I was forced to move out. Second, some students kept harassing me by calling me all types of names.

"I think it is time to heal and accept who we are. I don't know if I'll see tomorrow, but I hope that we, as gay students, are able to have normal lives like everybody else."

After the meeting, there was a vigil in remembrance of others who had been persecuted due to their sexual orientation.

Chapter Twenty-Two

At the age of twenty-four, Manouska began to experience certain changes in his/her life. As she was teaching high school, she met another teacher whom she expressed his/her interest in. Many people started to question her impetuous actions. The headmaster noticed that Manouska had changed and he posed some questions as well.

"Manouska, how is the teaching?" he asked. "Do you have any concerns regarding the class? Do you have any needs that I need to help you with?"

Manouska started crying, and the headmaster handed her some tissues. After a few minutes, Manouska told the headmaster that he/she was attracted to this other teacher, but he/she did not know what to do. The headmaster had known Manouska when he/she was attending the high school and knew her past. Finally the headmaster told Manouska, with a soft voice, to follow his/her heart. Then he asked him/her another question: "Do you think your dilemma will affect your performance as a teacher?"

"No," Manouska replied.

The same day, Manouska met with some students and lectured them about the difficulty of sexual identity.

"People with sexual differences struggle daily in our community and other places. For instance, lifestyle of gay students, hermaphrodites, and transgender individuals is not acceptable in some communities. Sexual identity is a big crisis in our school. Some students are harassed, some commit suicide, and some are depressed. The question one should ask is why is it like this and who started this movement?"

One student replied that the community had no idea how to handle people who have different sexual orientation. Therefore, hermaphrodites, gay, and transgender students were victimized. After this discussion, Manouska concluded by saying "Despite the sexual preferences of anybody, others should respect and tolerate a hermaphrodite, gay, and transgender lifestyle." He/she continued by saying "Hermaphrodites did not make a choice."

Chapter Twenty-Three

Manouska's body began to change, and he/she became more female than male. Many in the high school could see Manouska as a woman instead of a man, and he/she continued to have the same interest for the other high school teacher. Manouska wore women's clothes, and he/she began to experience changes in his/her breasts, voice, and other parts of the body.

Manouska mother advised him/her not to stop her teaching career and not stop helping others who are experiencing sexual identity dilemma. He/she went to the same psychiatrist that he/she used to see when he/she was a child, and the psychiatrist advised Manouska to see a gynecologist. A week later, Manouska went to see the family gynecologist to find out why his/her body was changing. At the gynecologist's office, Manouska was crying and feeling depressed because he/she had no idea how to deal with the transformation of his/her body.

A few hours later, Manouska was called to go to the back so the gynecologist could see him/her. While there, the gynecologist told Manouska that the female hormone was taking over the male hormone, and all the changes he/she was experiencing had to do with the shrinking of the male body part; he/she would be completely female once the transformation was complete.

Manouska asked the gynecologist if he/she could date or be in a relationship with a man.

"It is up to the other person and you, Manouska," the gynecologist replied.

After the office visit, Manouska went back home and explained to his/her mother what had happened at the gynecologist clinic. His/her mother explained to him/her that life is unpredictable and that life is a journey rather than a destination. Regardless of the outcome, she said she would stand by Manouska and support him/her.

A week later, some parents in the community expressed concern about Manouska's lifestyle and how influential he/she had become in the community as a teacher. That same week the daily newspaper, *La Revolution*, commented on people's sexual orientation and the commentary went like this:

How do people react to sexual orientation? Every parent needs to be concerned about his child's sexual orientation. Despite a child's sexual orientation, parents should love their children. Parents may feel ashamed or embarrassed after finding out that their children are not heterosexual, but they need to accept their children as they are.

A child should be raised to be whomever he or she chooses and the child shouldn't have to display his or her sexual orientation to others. The problem that we all face in the community is the fear of unknown. Most parents seem to think that children with different sexual orientation are contagious, but this kind of thinking is not going to help the community to advance in a harmonious way.

The next day, people called the radio talk show to express their feelings about the newspaper commentary. Some were very happy with the commentary, and others voiced their opinion and refused to tolerate this type of acceptance in the community.

Chapter Twenty-Four

When Manouska was twenty-six, the news came out that, in a few months, Manouska would marry the man that he/she had met while teaching. The wedding was scheduled to take place on December 31, 1988.

Some people were outraged after hearing the news. Some said that because Manouska was neither male nor female and he/she should not be married to a man. Some said that marriage is between a man and a woman and objected to the wedding taking place in the community.

Many asked, "Will the marriage ever take place?"

Friends, students and families went to visit Manouska and offered him/her their support. It was an intense year. Some people were happy for him/her, and others kept asking many questions, like: Will these two have kids? Or will they adopt kids.

Many called the daily radio talk show to express their views.

"The world is coming to an end," some said. "Parents should not let their children go near these two people."

One caller, however, expressed his view that "Manouska and his or her partner should adopt children after their wedding. Manouska has the right to love whoever he/she wants to love, and others should not be judgmental."

The wedding did not take place on December 31, 1988. What happened? During that same year, Manouska experienced symptoms of muscle weakness in her hands, arms, and legs and had difficulty swallowing and breathing. Manouska went to see his/her family doctor. After running so many tests, the doctor called Manouska and let him/her know that he/she had Amyotrophic Lateral Sclerosis (ALS) and that his/her case was very progressive.

The news shocked Manouska, his/her family, and his/her friends.

Chapter Twenty-Five

For Manouska, there was no hope. His/her wedding was cancelled due to the disease. Every day was a challenge.

Many kept asking is what ALS is. It is a degenerative disease affecting the human nervous system. It mangles people due to a failure in the body's motor neurons, which are nerve cells in the brainstem and spinal cord that control muscle contractions. In ALS, these neurons decline as the disease progresses to an advanced stage. Early symptoms of ALS include dropping things. Twitching or cramping of muscles and abnormal fatigue of the arms and legs may soon follow, causing difficulty with daily activities, such as walking or dressing. In more advanced stages, however, shortness of breath or difficulty in breathing and swallowing ensue, until the body is completely taken over by the disease.

Families and friends offered their daily support to Manouska after the diagnosis. People in the neighborhood sympathized and empathized with him/her. Many kept saying that he/she was too young to catch this disease.

Manouska's mother took him/her to a specialist for a second opinion regarding ALS. While they were waiting for the specialist, Manouska told his/her mother that he/she felt weak and that he/she was not able to breathe. A few minutes later, the receptionist called Manouska to go to the back and wait for the doctor. After many tests, the doctor told Manouska and his/her mother that the disease was very progressive and Manouska would need help with daily activities. The doctor prescribed medication and oxygen for Manouska, as well as use of a wheelchair so he/she could move around the house and other places.

As the disease progressed, Manouska had more difficulty breathing and was unable to walk. He/she lived in excruciating pain daily. Manouska experienced depression and thoughts of suicide every day. His/her mother watched his/her daily activity while using the wheelchair.

One day, Manouska's mother went to see a friend who lived nine hours away from the city to find out if she could get help for Manouska. When she got home, she went to Manouska's room and found that he/she was unresponsive. She called for help, but it was too late.

Manouska committed suicide by overdosing on drugs in January 1990.

Chapter Twenty-Six

It was the most depressing day for many in the neighborhood. Neighbors, friends, families, and students expressed their sorrow and grief. The high school's flag was lowered, and many teachers offered their condolences.

On the day of his/her funeral, many came to pay homage to Manouska. At the exposé, many speeches were given. One speech went like this:

"Comradeship is one of the most cherished things in people's lives. Most of us had the bliss of befriending Manouska when he or she moved to the community. We have appreciated him or her and despised him or her at times and found out how great he or she was. He or she was compassionate and caring. Manouska was a friend to many of us. For many of us in the high school, we could go to him/her when there was a problem.

"One day," said the speaker, "I was really depressed, and Manouska came to my supported me and stayed with me until I felt better. He or she stood up for what was right.

"Many in the community discriminated against people with different sexual orientations, but Manouska showed these people that we are all human beings with real flesh and blood.

"No matter what, Manouska was always there to support others when times where bad. He or she might not share the same values and dreams, but he or she was someone that most of us would like to have around.

"I know some of us were fortunate to know such a stunning and gifted person. It has been a blessing to know Manouska. Our friend will be missed and will be in our hearts forever."

Many in the community had feared that the life of Manouska would transform other children's lives, and they were wrong. However, the life and death of Manouska brought the community together and taught many valuable lessons.

Do not discriminate against others because of their sexual orientation or lifestyle.

Accept others despite their differences.

Stand up for your rights.

Do not live in fear of persecution.

Respect and love others despite their preferences.

Follow your instinct, and do not let others steal your dreams.

Do not be a quitter.

The Last Word

I believe we all have a part to play in our communities. Each and every one of us affects someone in our community, either positively or negatively. We won't always realize our influence on others unless it is pointed out to us.

In most communities, we judge others by the type of car they drive, the type of house they live in, the type of clothes they wear, and the type of friends they have. We also judge others because they are different. After analyzing the life and death of Manouska, many of us need to step back and ask the questions: How can I make a difference in my community? Do I judge others because of their sexual preference or by their actions?

We need to understand that homosexuals, hermaphrodites, transgender individuals are people like us. There is no need to be afraid of them. Our communities would be better places if we all developed peaceful relationships with others.